Moments with Angels

Moments with Angels

by
Robert Strand

New Leaf Press

First printing: March 1996
Fifth printing: October 1999

ISBN: 0-89221-324-8
Library of Congress Number: 95:73135

All Scripture references are from the New International Version, unless otherwise noted.

Every effort has been made to locate the authors or originators of the stories contained in this book. Most are the result of conversations with pastors, while others were accumulated throughout the course of a 30-year radio and television broadcasting career.

Please visit our website for other great titles:
www.newleafpress.net

Presented to:

_____

_____

Presented by:

_____

_____

Date:

_____

_____

Day 1
About Angels

Everybody knows about angels . . . well, at least on some level. And it seems that more people are talking about angels than ever before. Today there are boutiques devoted to angels, and greeting cards, poetry, songs, and books portraying them in all their goodness. We even take these wonderful "angelic" qualities and apply them to a sweetheart, spouse, kids, or special people.

Billy Graham, in his popular book on angels, states, "Angels have a much more important place in the Bible than the devil and his demons."[1] The Bible is chock-full of dramatic angelic appearances . . . Abraham, Jacob, Moses, Joshua, Gideon, David, Elijah, Zechariah, Joseph, Mary, and Peter, along with others, saw angels. Angels in the Bible are seen in many roles . . . climbing ladders, wrestling with people, taming lions, lifting great weights, announcing births, recruiting leaders, warriors in battle, executioners, performing miraculous rescues, and comforting people.

Two angels are mentioned by name . . . Michael and Gabriel. Michael is depicted in three biblical books as the "Great Prince" or archangel; Gabriel is shown as presiding over paradise.

So what are angels? We know, according to the Bible, that they are created beings, dignified, majestic, and intelligent. They are personal beings who always represent God but are not omnipresent, which God is. Little is said of their appearance, but they can take on the physical form of a person and sometimes are mistaken for another human being. The word "angel" simply means "messenger." They are seen as protectors, messengers ordered by God to minister in a myriad of ways in the Bible.

Some things to note: At no time should an angel or angels be worshiped! The Bible is very clear that only God is to be worshiped. Second, we are not to pray to angels! You might ask God for help in an emergency, but we are never to pray to angels. Let's open our eyes and ears of understanding and ask God to help us develop a healthy balance in regard to His angels.

This book is a collection of "angel" stories . . . to my knowledge all of the following are presented as true, factual, real-life stories. They have not been researched beyond the accounts of the people who experienced them. The stories are taken at face value as shared. I believe that angels exist! You be the judge. Read on and rejoice!

Today's Quote: *Angels are "incorporated spirits created by God to worship Him and carry out His will."* — Billy Graham

Today's Verse: For by Him all things were created: things in heaven and on earth, visible and invisible, whether thrones or powers or rulers or authorities; all things were created by Him and for Him (Col. 1:16).

Day 2
Angels on Assignment

This happened in 1956 during the Mau Mau uprisings in East Africa and is told by Phil Plotts, son of missionary Morris Plotts:

A band of roving Mau Maus came to the village of Lauri, surrounded it and killed every inhabitant including women and children . . . 300 in all. Not more than three miles away was the Rift Valley School, a private school where missionary children were being educated. Immediately upon leaving the carnage of Lauri, they came with spears, bows and arrows, clubs, and torches to the school with the same intentions of complete destruction in mind.

Of course, you can imagine the fear of those little inhabitants along with their instructors housed in the boarding school. Word had already reached them about Lauri. There was no place to flee with little children and women. So their only resource was to go to prayer.

Out of the darkness of the night, lighted torches appeared. Soon there was a complete ring of these terrorists around the school. Shouting and curses could be heard coming from the Mau Maus. Then they began to advance. All of a sudden, when they got close enough to throw spears, they stopped! Then began to run! A call had gone out to the authorities and an army had been sent but arrived after the Mau Maus had run. The army then spread out searching, which led to the capture of the entire band of raiders. Later, before the judge at their trial, the leader was called to the witness stand. The judge questioned: "On this particular night, did you kill the inhabitants of Lauri?"

"Yes."

"Was it your intent to do the same at the missionary school in Rift Valley?"

"Yes."

"Well, then," asked the judge, "why did you not complete your mission? Why didn't you attack the school?"

Remember . . . this was a heathen person from the darkness who had never read the Bible or heard about angels. The leader of the Mau Maus said: "We were on our way to attack and destroy all the people and school . . . but as we came closer, all of a sudden, between us and the school there were huge men dressed in white with flaming swords, and we became afraid and ran to hide."

Today's Quote: *When angels come, the devils leave.* — Ancient Proverb

Today's Verse: For He will command His angels concerning you to guard you in all your ways; they will lift you up in their hands, so that you will not strike your foot against a stone (Ps. 91:11-12).

Day 3
Angel in the Pool

It was a hot, humid summer day in the Midwest. Jamie went to one of his friend's homes to spend the early afternoon in the pool. It was great to spend time with the old gang and the swimming and diving and horse-play was fun. Reluctantly he left to do his summer job.

Later that night, he had a date with Jennifer in a neighboring town. As Jamie drove home he noticed the night, it was special . . . stars and moon had disappeared. The hot summer's day seemed to have permeated the night and almost cast a spell of darkness and humidity over the countryside. It was still hot and muggy, just perfect for a late night swim to cool off. On his way home, he passed his friend's home and decided to take a midnight swim. It was late, the house was dark. He was welcome to use the pool, but didn't want to awaken anybody in the house . . . as he quietly made his way through the back yard, he imagined how good the cool water would feel on a hot, muggy night that only other midwesterners can identify with.

Jamie quickly changed into his swimsuit in the pool cabana and climbed the diving board, paused, then was poised to make his dive head first into the pool. As he looked down into the pool, shrouded in darkness . . . he looked again. There beneath him, in the pool was something he'd never seen before. There was something that glowed with brilliance, sort of in the shape of a cross. He saw what looked like something glimmering in the darkness below. He thought, *Maybe it looks like an angel.*

Never taking his eyes off the silvery, shimmering, brilliant form, he slowly climbed back down the ladder of the diving board and walked to the edge of the pool for a closer look. When he knelt down to look closer . . . this thing was gone! Just disappeared! Gone! He was positive it could have been an angel. Then Jamie realized that he was looking into a swimming pool with no water in it!

When he stopped back by the next day he learned that his friend's parents had drained the pool after the guys had finished swimming in it the previous day so that cleaning and repairs could be done to it. It's with fond memories that Jamie recalls that special summer night when an angel saved his life . . . or at the least from a life-changing, crippling, head, back, or neck injury. It could have been fatal.

Today's Quote: *Those who are readiest to trust God without evidence other than His Word, always receive the greatest number of visible evidences of His love.* — C. G. Trumbull

Today's Verse: Even though I walk through the valley of the shadow of death, I will fear no evil, for You are with me; Your rod and Your staff, they comfort me (Ps. 23:4).

Day 4
No Angels

You think there are no angels any more . . .
No angels come to tell us in the night
Of joy or sorrow, love or death.
No breath of wings, no touch of palm to say
Divinity is near.
Today
Our revelations come
By telephone, or postman at the door.
You say . . .
Oh no, the hour when fate is near,
Not these the voices that can make us hear.
Not these
Have power to pierce below the stricken mind,
Deep down into perception's quivering core.
Blows fall unheeded on the bolted door;
Deafly we listen; blindly look; and still
Our fingers fumbling with the lock are numb,
Until
The Angels come.
Oh, do you not recall

It was a tree,
Springing from earth so passionately straight
And tall,
That made you see, at last, what giant force
Lay pushing in your heart?
And was it not that spray
Of dogwood blossoms, white across your road,
That all at once made grief too great a load to bear?
No angels any more, you say,
No towering sword, no angry seas divide . . .
No angels . . .
But a single bud of quince,
Flowering out of season on the day
She died,
Cracked suddenly across a porcelain world!

(Anne Morrow Lindbergh)

Today's Quote: *Angels mean messengers and ministers. Their function is to execute the plan of divine providence, even in earthly things.*
— Thomas Aquinas

Today's Verse: See, I am sending an angel ahead of you to guard you along the way and to bring you to the place I have prepared (Exod. 23:20).

Day 5
Protection in Israel

The Reverend Frankie Walker, a traveling evangelist, related the following story.

I was released from a Bible school in Virginia in August of 1990 to go to my next assignment in Israel. The Gulf War was threatening to go full-scale and Saddam Hussein was a great threat to Israel at this time. President Bush had encouraged the American people to stay away from Israel. It was not uncommon to have two or three tourist cars blown up each week and many senseless killings, especially of the blue-eyed, blonde-hair people . . . Americans or those who looked like Americans. The importance of missionaries to be led and guided by the Holy Spirit was a major factor in their protection.

I was not afraid the whole three and one-half months I was there, but I was always in tune with the leading of the Holy Spirit and sensed the presence of angels with me at all times.

This experience, only one of many, was to do with Jerusalem. I traveled there from Rehovot, where I lived while there. It was approximately an hour's bus ride. I had gone to Jerusalem many times and stayed there, sometimes for days at a time.

I had not been able to go the Upper Room, where all Christians want to go, because of the danger. I was determined to make a visit there, nevertheless. One Sunday after church I headed for the Damascus Gate and just before the street I was to turn down to go there, I had a strong impression not to go and to go instead to the YMCA for tea. I had learned to rely on such promptings so I immediately proceeded to the YMCA. I ordered tea and had sat there for a short time when some people from Europe came and sat at the table next to me. In a loud and clear voice I overheard one man say, "I'm glad we were not inside the Damascus Gate when the riots broke out." Then another added, "They had all those homemade bombs and the knives and rocks were flying and they destroyed the police booth and locked out the police that came to reinforce the soldiers who were inside."

Praise welled up inside of me. If I had not been in tune with the Spirit, I could have been injured or killed, because many were hurt and several killed that day.

Obedience is a must for all of God's children who might travel to dangerous places, because your very life may depend upon it.

Today's Quote: *Half of Americans . . . and three-fourths of teenagers-believe in angels.* — 1990 Gallup Poll

Today's Verse: The Son of Man will send out His angels, and they will weed out of His kingdom everything that causes sin and all who do evil (Matt. 13:41).

Day 6
If You Want to
See the Angels

Have YOU ever seen an angel? Dr. S. W. Mitchell, a Philadelphia neurologist, thought he had. After one very tiring day he retired early, but was awakened by a persistent knocking at the door. It was a little girl, poorly dressed and deeply upset. She told him that her mother was very sick and needed his help. Even though it was a bitterly cold, snowy night, Mitchell dressed and followed the girl.

He found the mother desperately ill with pneumonia. After treating her, Dr. Mitchell complimented the sick woman on her daughter's persistence and courage. The woman said, "My daughter died a month ago. Her shoes and coat are in the closet there."

Dr. Mitchell went to the closet and opened the door. There hung the very coat worn by the little girl who had been at his front door. The coat was warm and dry and could not possibly have been out in the wintry night!

Have YOU ever seen an angel?

One night the king of Syria sent his army under cover of darkness with lots of chariots and horses and horsemen to surround the city and cut off all escape routes. When the prophet and his servant got up early the next morning and checked around outside, they discovered troops, horses, and chariots everywhere! The servant, obviously frightened, asked, "Now what are we going to do?"

Elisha the prophet answered in so many words, "Don't be afraid because our army is larger than theirs!" Then, Elisha prayed, "Lord, open his eyes and let him see." And when the Lord had opened the young man's eyes he saw horses of fire and chariots of fire everywhere on the mountains surrounding the army which had surrounded them!

Have YOU ever seen an angel? Maybe we just need our eyes to be opened!

Today's Quote: *The guardian angels of life sometimes fly so high as to be beyond our sight, but they are always looking down upon us.* — Jean Paul Richter

Today's Verse: And Elisha prayed, "O Lord, open his eyes so he may see." Then the Lord opened the servant's eyes, and he looked and saw the hills full of horses and chariots of fire all around Elisha (2 Kings 6:17).

Day 7
Jackie's Angel

Jackie is a beautiful girl of 17 with shining black hair and sparkling brown eyes. A delightful glow sets her apart from other beautiful young girls.

Three years ago Jackie faced a painful tragedy. Doctors had discovered a tumor on her cheekbone . . . the kind of tumor usually found only on a long bone such as an arm or leg. It had spread its deadly tentacles throughout the entire cheek region of her attractive face. Surgery offered the only hope to save Jackie's life. The doctors would be making an incision along the nose area and down through the upper lip. All of her teeth on the left side of her face would have to be removed as well as the cheekbone, the nose bone, and the jaw bone. Needless to say, an operation of this immensity, performed on the face of a lovely, at that time 14-year-old girl, was a grim prospect. Many tears were shed.

Several days before the surgery, lying in her hospital bed, she thought about what it would mean to go through life so terribly scarred, if indeed she even lived through the operation. She was frightened, she desperately wanted to live. She wanted to experience all that life held for her. As she tossed on her pillow in lonely fear that night, she began to pray. With tears of anxious apprehension, she asked God to help her.

About two o'clock in the morning Jackie was awakened. She didn't know what woke her up; she only knew she was awake and alert. She saw a glowing light at the foot of her bed, and the silvery form of an angel appeared. The presence was very powerful and totally loving. An aura of stillness filled Jackie like the warmth of a summer day. She felt enfolded by the presence and a sense of incredible wonder touched every part of her body.

A voice filled with sunshine said, "Do not be afraid, Jackie. You are going to be all right." And then the angel presence was gone.

The following day, Jackie was taken to the X-ray room for preoperative X-rays. To the utter astonishment of the doctors, every trace of the tumor and its deadly tentacles was gone!

That was three years ago. Now here she is, this beautiful daffodil princess. Her lovely face is unmarred, and she remains very much aware of God's miraculous touch upon her life![2]

Today's Quote: *To the heavenly angels, who possess God in humility and serve Him in blessedness, all material nature and all rational life are subject.* — Saint Augustine

Today's Verse: But the angel said to them, "Do not be afraid. I bring you good news of great joy" (Luke 2:10).

Day 8
The Vanishing Hitchhiker

While researching for this book on angels . . . one recurring kind of story popped up everywhere with all kinds of variations or adaptations. Practically every publication about angels will have a version and most people you ask can tell you about somebody they know who has had such an experience. Perhaps it could be called the "classic" automobile angel legend/story. It usually goes something like this.

A girl and her father were driving along a country road on their way home from their cabin when they saw a young lady hitchhiking. They stopped and picked her up and she got in the back seat. She told the girl and her father that she lived in a house about five miles up the road. She didn't say anything, but sat and watched out the window. When the father saw the house, he drove up to it and turned around to tell the girl they had arrived . . . but she wasn't there!

Both he and his daughter were mystified and knocked on the door to tell the people what had happened. They in turn told them that they once had a daughter who answered the description of the girl they supposedly had picked up, but she had disappeared some years ago and had last been seen hitchhiking on this very road.

Or it can be heard much like this: Pastor Hernandez was on his way to make a call on a sick member of his church. It was a 15-mile desolate stretch of barren land when he stopped to pick up a young hitchhiker. As they drove along, the pastor began to share with the young man about the love of Jesus Christ.

Pastor Hernandez specifically said in the course of conversation, "I believe the Lord's return is getting very close."

The young man softly, yet forcefully, replied, "Well, that will be sooner than you think." Which was a surprise to the pastor.

They continued to drive further and the young man continues, "Please make sure you are ready and all of your congregation also gets this warning."

The pastor now contemplates this message, feeling some kind of special occurrence is happening. He keeps his eyes on the road.

But when the pastor turns to look at his passenger, the young man is gone! He stops the car, gets out, and looks up and down the lonely road but is unable to see anyone in any direction!

Do you think the frequency of this story is a message to us who are living in what may be called "the last days"?

Today's Quote: *He has His reasons for doing what He does, and He will explain them to us someday.* — Emidio John Pepe

Today's Verse: Whether you turn to the right or to the left, your ears will hear a voice behind you, saying, "This is the way; walk in it" (Isa. 30:21).

Day 9
God's Special Messenger

In the spring of 1982 I was the speaker at a morning prayer group which meets in a town near Springfield, Illinois. Before I spoke, a neighboring pastor shared about his recent trip to Mexico.

He, along with several others, had gone there on a preaching mission. While they were returning, their van developed mechanical problems. After jacking up the van, the pastor crawled underneath to check out the problem. The jack collapsed, and he suddenly felt the crushing weight of the van on his chest. His companions quickly grabbed the bumper to lift the van. They weren't able to budge it. He cried out, "Jesus! Jesus!" Within a few seconds a youthful-looking man came running toward them. He was thin and small in stature. He was smiling. As he reached them, he grabbed the van and lifted it. The others joined in, and the van lifted like a feather.

As he was freed, the pastor felt his chest expand and the broken bones mend. The visitor then lowered the van, waved to them, and ran in the direction from which he had come until he disappeared on the horizon. No one knew who the mysterious visitor was or where he had come from![3]

Of all the personalities or supernatural beings talked about in the Bible, it's the angels who are most constantly depicted as being completely identified with heaven. As you read through the Bible and look up the angel stories, you will read such things as when the angel of the Lord called to Hagar in the wilderness "from heaven."

Then there is the time when Jacob saw angels at Bethel . . . there he saw a ladder reaching to heaven on which the angels of God were ascending and descending. In many other places the angels are named the "heavenly ones" or the "heavenly host."

When the angelic choir had finished their special song for the shepherds at the announcement of the birth of Jesus Christ, it says that they "went away into heaven." It was an angel "from heaven" who came and rolled away the stone from the tomb of Jesus. And it was our Lord himself who spoke often of "the angels in heaven." Angels make one of the most interesting biblical studies!

Today's Quote: *All night, all day, Angels watching over me, my Lord.* — "ALL NIGHT, ALL DAY," a traditional song

Today's Verse: Then King Nebuchadnezzar leaped to his feet in amazement and asked his advisers, "Weren't there three men that we tied up and threw into the fire?" They replied, "Certainly, O king." He said, "Look! I see four men walking around in the fire, unbound and unharmed, and the fourth looks like a son of the gods" (Dan. 3:24-25).

Day 10
A Summons to the Danger Zone

Nurse Edie Murphy worked at a state psychiatric hospital in Massachusetts. Such a job is challenging, and one of the hardest parts is admitting new patients being brought in by ambulance. "You're never sure what state they're in, if they're violent, for instance," she says. Ambulances discharged patients in a deserted basement area. Procedure involved *two* people meeting the ambulance, an admitting nurse and a male mental-health technician.

One night Edie was helping out in a ward other than her own, when she learned that a patient was on his way by ambulance. Because everyone else was busy, Edie volunteered to meet him. "I was uneasy because I rarely did admissions, and the technician who accompanied me was new and very hesitant," she says. However, as the two came down the quiet corridor, Edie saw Dan waiting for them. This was a relief, since Dan was a strong and reliable tech with whom she had often worked. What a nice coincidence! The ambulance drove up, deposited the patient, and left.

"Hi, I'm Edie Murphy." Edie smiled at the young man who she later learned was psychotic. "I'll be doing your admission." She watched as his expression began to change. This could be a dangerous point, when a patient realized he was going to be hospitalized.

Without warning, the young man lunged at Edie, grabbing for her throat. Dan, instantly alert, caught the patient in a basket-hold and subdued him while Edie summoned additional help.

Her heart was still racing an hour later when she and Dan discussed the close call. "I'm so glad you were there," Edie told him.

"It was lucky you phoned," Dan agreed. "But how did you know I was working overtime, and five buildings away from you?"

Edie frowned. "What do you mean? I didn't call you."

"But. . . " Dan stared at her. "Some woman phoned our medical-room nurse. She said, 'Send Dan to Admissions. Edie needs help.' "

Some woman . . . but who? The busy nurses on Edie's floor hadn't phoned. They had already sent an escort with Edie and were not aware Dan was still on duty. The nurses on Dan's ward didn't know Edie or anything about a new admission. When the phone rang, that nurse was in the usually vacant cubbyhole, pouring a medication.

Who summoned Dan before Edie had even arrived?[4]

Today's Quote: *Angels may not always come when you call them, but they come when you need them.* — Karen Goldman

Today's Verse: In speaking of the angels He says, "He makes His angels winds, His servants flames of fire" (Heb. 1:7).

Day 11
The Messenger

Yvonne (name changed) was 17, pregnant, penniless, and afraid. She was at her wits' end not knowing what to do. As she sat, tearfully watching the sonogram of her baby, she saw the new life, alive and moving, and knew in that moment that an abortion would be out of the question for this helpless new life. Nightly, she cried herself to sleep.

Then, one night an angel appeared to her in a dream. It said, "Don't be afraid. Everything will be fine because you and your baby will be well taken care of."

The angel pulled back the curtain and gave her a look into the future. Yvonne watched as her baby, healthy, strong, and beautiful was placed by the angel into the arms of a wonderful, caring, loving couple. The next scene showed the baby as a grown woman, mature and happy. The angel told her God was concerned about the baby and would work it all out for good for her as-yet-unborn child. Then the angel turned to Yvonne and touched her with a light that seemed to give off a warm glow that stayed with Yvonne in her heart.

As Yvonne awoke the next morning she felt wonderful, loved, and that everything would be worked out for the best. On this same day she was introduced to a lady who told her about a support group/home for unwed mothers. The next day Yvonne found herself in attendance with this support group where she found healing for her emotions and help about the choices she could make as to her baby's future.

Her choice was to give birth and place the child with a Christian adoption agency. While she held her baby for the last time, Yvonne had her own dedication ceremony for her baby.

In Yvonne's story the angel appeared in a dream with a message. There is also a biblical story which parallels hers. About 2,000 years ago an angel appeared in a dream to a man named Joseph with instructions about another unborn child, even to giving him the child's name. Later, this same man, Joseph, had another dream in which an angel gave him the message that he was to take the young child to Egypt to escape the plans of King Herod, who intended to kill Jesus. The word "angel" in the Greek language originally means a "messenger."

Today's Quote: *To comfort and to bless, to find a balm for woe, to tend the lone and fatherless, is angels' work below.* — W. W. How

Today's Verse: But after he had considered this, an angel of the Lord appeared to him in a dream and said, "Joseph son of David, do not be afraid to take Mary home as your wife, because what is conceived in her is from the Holy Spirit. She will give birth to a son, and you are to give him the name Jesus, because he will save his people from their sins" (Matt. 1:20-21).

Day 12
The Train Stops Just in Time

The crack British express train raced through the night, its powerful head lamp spearing the darkness ahead. This was a special run because it was carrying Queen Victoria and her attendants.

Suddenly . . . the engineer saw a startling sight! Revealed in the powerful beam of the engine's headlights was a weird figure loosely wrapped in a black coat that was flapping in the breeze, standing on the middle of the train tracks, waving its arms, a signal to stop! The engineer immediately grabbed for the brakes and brought the train to a screeching, grinding, sparks-flying halt!

Then the engineer, his assistant, the coal tender, and a couple of conductors climbed down to see what had stopped them. They looked, but they could find no trace of the strange figure. But on a hunch, the engineer walked a few yards further down the tracks. Instantly he stopped and stared into the fog in horror! The rain storm, which passed through the area earlier in the evening, had caused the bridge to wash out in the middle span and it had toppled into the storm-swollen stream! If he had not paid attention to the ghostly, weird figure, the train would have plunged into the overflowing stream . . . with, how many lives lost or bodies mangled, who knows? The engineer was so overcome with the emotion of the near miss that he sat down on the tracks for a few moments before making his way back to the idling steam engine.

Word was wired for help. And while the bridge and tracks were being repaired, the crew again made a more intensive search for the strange flagman, unsuccessfully. But it wasn't until they got to London that the mystery was solved.

At the base of the steam engine's head lamp, the engineer discovered a huge dead moth. He looked at it a few moments . . . then, on impulse, wet its wings and pasted it to the glass of the head lamp.

Climbing back into the cab . . . he switched on the lamp and saw the "flagman" in the beam. He knew the answer now, the moth had flown into the beam mere seconds before the train was due to reach the washed-out bridge. In the fog it had appeared to be a phantom figure, a flagon waving its arms signaling the train to stop!

Later when Queen Victoria was told of the strange happenings she said, "I'm sure it was no accident. It was God's way of protecting us."

Today's Quote: *We know little of their constant ministry. The Bible assures us, however, that one day our eyes will be unscaled to see and know the full extent of the attention angels have given us.* — Billy Graham

Today's Verse: Praise the Lord, you His angels, you mighty ones who do His bidding, who obey His word (Ps. 103:20).

Day 13
Miracle Under the Hood

Often the origins of a story can't be traced. Such is this one which had been told to a nationwide TV audience by the late Howard Conatser, founder of the Beverly Hills Baptist Church of Dallas.

The names are lost, so we'll just call these two teenage sisters Cheriee and Susan. They had been shopping in a suburban mall. When they were ready to go home, it was dark, too late! From the exit they saw their car, the only one left in that section of the parking lot.

They were nervous . . . waiting, hoping some other customers would come along so they could all walk out together. They were aware of the current crime wave in area shopping malls and remembered Dad's warning: "Don't stay too late!"

"Let's get with it . . . now!" Susan shifted her packages, pushed open the door and walked as fast as she could with Cheriee following, both looking from side to side. They just made it! Cheriee shoved the key into the door lock, got in, reached across to open Susan's door. THEN . . . they both heard the sound of running feet behind them. They turned to look and panicked — racing toward their car were two ominous looking men! One of the men shouted, "We got you, you're not going anywhere!"

Susan jumped in and both locked their doors just in time.

With shaking hands, Cheriee turned the ignition switch. Nothing! She tried again and again . . . nothing! Click! Silence! No power! The men were ready to smash a window.

The girls knew there were scant seconds of safety left . . . they joined hands and prayed! "Dear God," Susan pleaded, "give us a miracle in the name of Jesus!"

Again Cheriee turned the key . . . the engine roared to life and they raced out of the lot!

The girls cried all the way home, shocked and relieved. They screeched into the driveway, pulled the car into the garage, burst into the house, spilling out their story to Mom and Dad. They held them both as they comforted two frightened daughters.

"You're safe . . . thank God, that's the main thing. But don't do it again," Dad said. Then their father frowned, "It's strange. That car has never failed to start. I'll just check it out. I'll take a look at it now."

In the garage he raised the hood . . . in one stunned glance, he realized WHO had brought his daughters home safely that night! There was no battery in the car!

Today's Quote: *When I pray, coincidences happen, when I stop praying, coincidences stop.* — William Temple

Today's Verse: The men were amazed and asked, "What kind of man if this? Even the winds and the waves obey Him!" (Matt. 8:27).

Day 14
Angels Unaware

In 1937 the Japanese began a full-scale invasion of China. In 1938 Dick and Margaret Hillis were missionaries for the China Inland Mission. By January of 1941 the Japanese were advancing toward their home in Shenkiu. Their city was soon to be the center of fighting. They had two small babies . . . two months and just over a year. In the midst of this Dick had an appendicitis attack with the closest doctor 115 miles away. What to do.

Miraculously, God had kept them safe and the Japanese did not invade this city. Dick packed them into two rickshaws to head for Shanghai. They were stopped at the Sand River by the Chinese army. They asked for permission to pass through the lines but the commander told them they were crazy. Eventually the commander gave them a written note of permission to go through the lines. As they were leaving the officer's headquarters, they were spotted by the son of a Christian they knew who recognized Dick. He was an opium smuggler, black sheep of the family, who offered them a place to sleep, a boat to cross the river, and a guide. God's first angel had come as a smuggler.

In the "no-man's land" they were approached by three Japanese officers. The one in the center was a two-star general. In perfect English he addressed Dick, "Where in the world did you come from?"

Dick was astonished . . . then quickly told his story of illness and the need for a hospital, rest, and milk. "And may I ask you, sir, where did you learn such perfect English?"

Without hesitation the officer informed them that he had attended the University of Washington in 1936. "General," Dick said, "give me the pleasure of introducing you to one of your fellow alumni. My wife was also at the University of Washington in 1936.

The General's face beamed. He greeted Margaret warmly and promised to fulfill each of their requests. "In the morning I will give you a pass to take you through Japanese lines. You will find milk at the little church, for the former missionary there owned a cow."[5]

And so God supplied three angels, who themselves, no doubt, were unaware of their role in guiding God's servant family to safety in a great time of trouble.

Today's Quote: *Open your ears and open your hearts and hear me well. You have never been forsaken. Nor was God far away from you, even in your darkest hour.* — Joseph F. Girzone

Today's Verse: The angel of the Lord encamps around those who fear Him, and He delivers them (Ps. 34:8).

Day 15
Three More Angel Short Stories

• DURING WW II Wayne was the navigator on a B-24 bomber and stationed in Italy. On one particular bombing run over central Europe, as they were approaching the target area, he felt a strong hand on his shoulder and a voice which said, "Get up and go to the back of the plane!" He immediately got up and in that brief time of walking to the back and returning they had taken some limited anti-aircraft fire. When Wayne took his place back in the cockpit, he noticed a shell had blown a hole in the ceiling of the plane and right through his navigator's seat!

• IN CHINA, a 70-year-old mother was the only one who had knowledge of most of the daily operations of the family as well as how the operations of their house church were carried out. She alone knew where the Bibles were hidden, who the messengers were, who could be trusted. Then, suddenly she died of a heart attack. Her family felt the loss. She had not been able to pass on to them the vital information that was so needed. So they began to pray, "Lord, restore our mother back to life!"

After being dead for two days she came back to life! She scolded her family for calling her back. They reasoned with her. They said they would pray that in two more days she could return to the Lord as it would take that much time to set all these matters straight. After two days, the family and friends began to worship the Lord and prayed that the Lord would take her back home. The mother's final words were, "They're coming! Two angels are coming!" And this incident caused an entire village to become Christian!

• SIX SOVIET COSMONAUTS said they witnessed a most awe-inspiring spectacle in space. They saw a band of glowing angels! According to *Weekly World News,* cosmonauts Vladimir Solovev, Oleg Atkov, and Leonid Kizim said they first saw the celestial beings during their 155th day aboard the orbiting "Salyat 7" space station. "What we saw," they said, "were seven giant figures in the form of humans, but with wings and mist-like halos, as in the classic depiction of angels." Twelve days later the figures returned and were seen by three other Soviet scientists, including woman cosmonaut Svetlann Savitskaya who said, "They were smiling, as though they shared in a glorious secret."

Today's Quote: *What he did see was light: light from the heavenly host as they swept the sky clean from one end to the other.* — Frank Peretti

Today's Verse: He then added, "I tell you the truth, you shall see heaven open, and the angels of God ascending and descending on the Son of Man" (John 1:51).

Day 16
Angel in the Snow

When you live in Colorado, especially in or near the mountains, or must cross them in the wintertime, you travel with precautions. What happens when you travel without precautions? Well, J.D. and his family are native to Colorado and live in Grand Junction on the western slope of the Rockies. They, in late August, had taken a trip and now were returning home and had to cross Red Mountain Pass from Durango to Grand Junction. It was still summertime and their car wasn't equipped for winter traveling as yet. They were making their climb over the pass which is 11,008 feet in elevation on the top. The highway is named the "Million Dollar Highway" because of the great cost per mile to build it originally. It's one of the most treacherous roads to travel because of the steep grades and hairpin turns. When weather is bad . . . wet or snowy or icy, the road is downright dangerous.

This family was traveling with three little kids. As they neared the top they noticed cloud cover and a storm brewing, but didn't think too much about it. But as they topped out at the summit and started down, immediately they found themselves in a late summer's snowstorm. Wind was blowing and snow was falling and freezing to an icy glaze on the roadway. There was no place to turn around or stop, no shelter, nothing to do but be as cautious as possible in attempting to navigate the now ice-covered, slick hairpin turns. I must also tell you that there are very few stretches where there are guardrails. Conditions worsened quickly. What to do? The first thing was to pray ... as J.D. drove, his wife Agnes and the kids were praying.

In spite of all careful precautions and gearing down, the car began to slip and slide. The edge, with no guardrail, was too close. The car continued to skid towards the edge with its thousands of feet to the valley below! ALL of a sudden, there appeared two men running beside the car ... one with his right hand on the front left fender and the other with his right hand on the left rear fender. The car straightened out of the skid and these two men continued to run alongside the car until it maneuvered the last treacherous, icy hairpin curve to enter the town of Ouray. They slowed and stopped so as to inquire and thank the men who had come to their rescue ... but there was no one to be found! There was no place to go but up or down the mountain road which was laid out before them. Safe, they expressed their thanksgiving to the Lord for His protection and whoever those two men were.

Today's Quote: *What's impossible to all humanity may be possible to the metaphysics and physiology of angels.* — Joseph Glanvill

Today's Verse: The angel of the Lord encamps around those who fear Him, and He delivers them (Ps. 34:7).

Day 17
The Restroom Angel

He was overdressed for the assignment and out of character for his immediate job! He was whistling while he toiled, smiling and greeting me as I ambled to my place.

This man was removing cigarette butts from the bathroom urinals, utilizing small scissors to retrieve the soggy and offensive stubs.

"That's not an envious job you're doing," I said.

"No Sir! No Sir! It's not! But it must be done. Looks bad when customers come into the bathroom. Makes people think we don't care or that we are not clean. So, I clean them up."

"Do men throw their cigarette butts in the urinals very often?" I inquired, as this well-dressed man checked the bathroom stalls.

"Often?! Every morning I pick several just out of one urinal."

"Why do people throw them in there?" I asked.

"Lazy, just lazy; or they don't care! Maybe they never were raised any better; maybe they have never grown up, perhaps they do it for meanness," he whispered determinedly under his breath. "And maybe they never had to clean up after themselves."

Upon leaving, I inquired, "You been working here long?"

I was startled out of idle chitchat when he replied, "I don't work here! I come here almost everyday. I have an office across the street."

"YOU WHAT??? You don't work here, and you clean up the bathroom? Why?"

"Because of the next man who comes in here and uses this place; I want him to notice the area is clean and that someone cares."

"Even if he throws a butt into your cleaned urinal?"

"Doesn't matter," said the stranger. "What counts is that this facility is clean for an hour, maybe two. And if the next man comes in here and notices this bathroom is clean, maybe he will comprehend the cleanness and leave the bathroom a better place when he walks out."

I washed my hands, tore paper from the towel dispenser, and found myself wiping up the extra water around the sink and cleaning the water droplets from the mirror. While throwing the paper towel into the garbage I picked up a piece of wet, used towel and placed it in the can.

Once outside I saw him walking and whistling his way out of the building, straightening his tie, sauntering across the street to his office.[6]

Today's Quote: *This world has angels all too few, and heaven is overflowing.* — Samuel Taylor Coleridge

Today's Verse: If I speak in the tongues of men and of angels, but have not love, I am only a resounding gong or a clanging cymbal (1 Cor. 13:1).

Day 18
The Warning

It was a typical school day morning. Ruthie Hoferman was making the regular drive with her two kids to Eugene Field Elementary School. The kids were doing their usual bickering and fighting on the short ride. This morning was different. Ruthie was attempting to cope with a migraine headache and so her patience was short.

Shouts kept coming from the backseat, "Mommie...he's grabbing my lunch box!" It was the scream of eight-year-old Lisa.

"Did not!" shouted back her nine-year-old son Robbie, with as much volume.

"Enough! Stop it!" Ruthie screamed into the back seat, "No more of it, both of you!" It was like shouting to the wind.

"There, he did it again!" cried Lisa.

Now...Ruthie gripped the wheel tighter, knuckles turning white, anger rising, prayed: "Please, Lord, help me make it this last half mile."

Quietly, then building, "Lisa is a tattletale! Lisa is a tattletale!!"

"He's teasing me! Make, him stop, Mommie!" came the shout from Lisa.

At that . . . Ruthie turned her head and scolded both kids vehemently! THEN . . . Ruthie distinctly heard a voice she had never heard before command: "Ruthie! Stop! Quick! Now!"

Stunned at the forcefulness of this strange voice, Ruthie quickly turned back to the road. There was a stop sign dead ahead! It was a four-way stop intersection. Slamming on her brakes, the car skidded, squealing to a violent stop. The seatbelts were the only restraint that kept the kids from being pitched into the front seat or windshield.

In mere nano-seconds after her stop . . . an old pickup loaded with trash plowed through the stop sign on her left at a high rate of speed. Then the driver lost control and veered hard right, hit the curb, and overturned, spilling its contents all over the street!

Other motorists rushed to help the pickup driver. Ruthie, still with the steering wheel in her white-knuckle grasp just sat there, then began to shake! One other driver approached her car, she cranked down the window and asked, "Is he hurt?"

"A little, more shook up than anything. He'll be all right." He added, "Lady, it's a good thing that you stopped when you did . . . that guy could have nailed you broadside. The angels sure must have been riding with you today, lady, is all I can say."

Today's Quote: *Any man who does not believe in miracles is not a realist.* — David Ben Gurion

Today's Verse: Whether you turn to the right or to the left, your ears will hear a voice behind you, saying, "This is the way; walk in it" (Isa. 30:21).

Day 19
Margarete's Angel

Two things are in short supply — well, it could be a whole lot more, when you are a college student — sleep, and money to go home on. Margarete was away at college, a hard working, diligent, college student, a sophomore. She stayed in the dormitory where sleep was a short commodity, too. Girls being girls and studies being studies and boys being subjects of conversation, the nights are pretty short.

The Christmas holidays were soon approaching which meant the trip home was in sight. But as always, college professors haven't much heart so they schedule tests on the last two or three days preceding vacation. So again sleep was hard to come by. Mom and Dad had sent the money for the bus ride home.

As soon as class was over on that Friday Margarete made her way to the depot, loaded with luggage and a few presents she had purchased. She bought her ticket and her choice seat was available, the last seat in the back, next to the back door where she could stretch out and sleep without interruption until her destination of Mankato, Minnesota!

What luxury . . . just to stretch out. The only sounds were those of people murmuring to each other and the tires on the highway, comforting, soothing sounds to lull a tired college sophomore to sleep. As she slept the bus motion and her tossing pushed her shoulders against the back door, then more of her body weight pressed against the door.

SUDDENLY without warning, the back door sprang open with Margarete pushed against it. She tipped out the door, head and shoulders first, awakening instantly with a start to feel herself falling into the blackness of the night towards the hard concrete. Her first thought was, *I'm about to die!* She grabbed for the door frame to catch herself but missed! She prayed a three word prayer, "Jesus help me!"

And to this day, she says she can almost still feel it . . . there was a pair of huge hands that caught her and pushed her back into the bus!

The bus driver, when the warning light came on, brought the bus to a quick stop and came running down the aisle to check on the problem. He came to Margarete and asked, "Are you all right? I can't understand how it happened. Did you lose anything?"

Still in shock, she answered, "No sir, no problems."

"How did you manage to hold on and not fall out?"

"I believe I had some heavenly help."

Today's Quote: *The most beautiful thing we can experience is the miraculous.* — Albert Einstein

Today's Verse: When you pass through the waters, I will be with you; and when you pass through the rivers, they will not sweep over you. When you walk through the fire, you will not be burned; the flames will not set you ablaze. For I am the Lord, your God, the Holy One of Israel, your Savior" (Isa. 43:2-3).

Day 20
Heavyweight Angels

My mother told me this story about another ministry couple who were contemporaries of theirs, the now deceased Pastor and Mrs. Bennie C. Heinz. At the time of this happening, the Heinz family was pastoring a North Dakota church.

Pastor and Mrs. Heinz and another couple made their way to a springtime fellowship meeting quite a distance away in the town of Dickinson. If I recall correctly, he was one of the speakers. This was one of those all-day affairs . . . morning service, lunch, afternoon service, minister's business meeting, dinner, and finally the evening rally/service. When they left it was approximately 10:30 p.m. as they drove away from the church. Weather in North Dakota can be very unpredictable in the springtime. They turned north on Highway 85 towards Williston and it started to rain/sleet/snow all at the same time.

They started down into the last valley and the icy mixture continued to fall, but with more intensity. It started to accumulate on the highway making driving very treacherous. They had no snow tires or chains on the car. Mrs. Heinz began to pray, "Help us Lord, help our car, keep us safe."

As they began the climb from the valley floor, the car began to lose traction and soon they came to a complete stop. No matter what was tried the car would spin out of control, no traction. Nothing to do but prepare to spend the night huddled in the car. About that time a car drove up behind them with six husky young men in it. They stopped behind the stalled car and one of them asked if they could be of help. Pastor Heinz said, "A push would help us but we really need more traction on the rear end, perhaps more weight would help."

The pastor started the car and five of these young men began to push the car up the steep road . . . after it got rolling they all jumped up on the trunk . . . two were hanging over the sides, the other three were sitting with their feet on the rear bumper. They easily made it.

At the top of the hill, Pastor Heinz stopped the car to get out to thank these kind heavyweight strangers. When he stepped out of the car to go to the rear to speak with the men . . . they were all gone! Disappeared! Not a trace! Not a track! Not even of the car in which they had come!

Today's Quote: *Reports continually flow to my attention from many places around the world telling of visitors of the angelic order appearing, ministering, fellowshiping, and disappearing.* — Billy Graham

Today's Verse: But you have come to Mount Zion, to the heavenly Jerusalem, the city of the living God. You have come to thousands upon thousands of angels in joyful assembly, to the church of the first born, whose names are written in heaven. You have come to God (Heb. 12:22-23).

Day 21
The Angel Customers

Robert today owns an over-the-road transport company, but before he got into the trucking business he had purchased a sporting goods store. He was the lone employee to start with. The store happened to be in an out-of-the-way part of town, sort of isolated, by itself.

One day while expressing his concerns to his pastor, the idea struck him to ask the pastor and some of the elders to come over and pray for the protection of Robert and his store. They also prayed that anyone who came to buy a gun for the wrong purposes would not be able to.

One afternoon a very tough, rough-looking character entered the store to buy a gun. Through the store-front window Robert saw that this man was accompanied by six or seven other equally tough-looking men on motorcycles now parked in front. Immediately Robert had the sense that this man did not have good intentions for purchasing a gun. So he refused to sell any guns or ammunition to this customer. The man left in an angry huff, jumped on his bike, motioned for the others to follow, made an obscene gesture through the window at Robert, and pealed out of the parking lot with tires squealing and pipes roaring.

The next morning this same man returned with his gang but didn't enter the store . . . they simply began circling the store on their bikes, no doubt, with the intent of intimidating Robert. They kept up this harassment most of the day. They would drive out of the lot and return again in a few minutes to circle the store again. All the while they would stare through the front window. Robert, alone in the store, began to pray: "Lord, help me. Please send your angels to protect me and keep the store safe from any harm."

After several hours of this harassment the leather-jacketed gang drove out of the lot . . . and never returned again!

Later, one of Robert's regular customers dropped by the store to visit. He mentioned that he'd been by earlier in the day but didn't bother to come in. Robert asked him why he hadn't.

"Well, because the inside of your store was packed full of customers. I knew you'd be so busy you wouldn't have time to visit with me," he replied.

Yet . . . NO ONE was in the store at any time that day!

Today's Quote: *There are no mistakes, no coincidences. All events are blessings given to us to learn from.* — Elisabeth Kubler-Ross

Today's Verse: Daniel answered, "O king, live forever! My God sent His angel, and he shut the mouths of the lions. They have not hurt me, because I was found innocent in his sight. Nor have I ever done any wrong before you, O king" (Dan. 6:21-22).

Day 22
The Messenger

This story begins in the early 1970s, in Rockford, Illinois, as Pastor Don Lyons led his church to purchase some farm land on which to build a church and a Christian radio station. They built a small house for the station's home, if they could get it launched. Pastor Lyons knew they needed a special person to manage the start up. As the pastor prayed about it . . . in his mind, he could see the name "Tietsort" spelled out. An unusual name. He dismissed it.

One day at a special pastor's meeting at which the churches in Rockford hosted a meeting, Pastor Lyons was greeting some of the guests when a young man walked up . . . the pastor stared at his name tag, "Ron Tietsort"! He was a pastor and had a radio/TV background in Sioux City, Iowa. Soon Ron accepted the job of station manager and moved his family.

His wife, Millie, became the bookkeeper, receptionist, and occasional programmer. Then in the winter of 1975 reality had to be faced. Despite all their efforts and a growing listener base, WQFL was in trouble. In order to catch up and keep it going, WQFL needed just over $3,000 and needed it like right NOW!

It might as well have been three million! Millie sat looking out the window on a new snowfall as she prayed, "God, we really thought

You wanted the station to succeed. Did we misread You? Please tell us what to do now."

The front door opened and a middle-aged man walked in, carrying a sealed envelope. Millie was startled . . . she'd heard no car in the drive, no footsteps on the porch. Perhaps the snow had muffled the sounds. "Give this to Ron. Use it for the station."

Before Millie could offer him a receipt for tax purposes he was gone. Strange.

She walked to Ron's desk, he slit the envelope open and gasped, "Millie, look!" Inside was more than $3,000 in cash! Ron leaped from his chair, raced to the front of the house, and flung open the door to call the man back so he could thank him or meet him.

BUT there was no car in the drive, no tire tracks in the driveway . . . none coming from the road and none going back. Then Ron looked down on the fresh snow of the porch which hadn't been shoveled yet, no tracks! No footprints on the white carpet anywhere!

Today WQFL and WGLS are still operating . . . and Ron and Millie never saw the stranger again. But they remember!

Today's Quote: *The farther we go along the path of God, the more angels we shall encounter.* — H. C. Moolenburgh

Today's Verse: And my God will meet all your needs according to His glorious riches in Christ Jesus (Phil. 4:19).

Day 23
Entertaining the Stranger

It happened in a southern state. Eugene and Judy had eight kids ranging in age from 5 to 15. They were a church-going, loving family. Gene had worked at a local lumber mill for years and when it folded he was left with doing odd jobs for a living. One day he had a small job in town working on a car. Judy on this day was doing the laundry when some church ladies dropped over for a visit.

Their conversation was broken when Judy's oldest came into the house, "Mom, there's a black man coming around to the back door. Says he's got to talk to you."

Immediately these church ladies warned, "Be careful. Don't have anything to do with a man who's comin' begging! Now hear!"

At the back door stood the elderly black man with greying hair and soft, warm eyes. "Ma'am, sorry to bother you, but my truck broke down and I'm walking to town. I would appreciate it if you could give me some water and just a bit of food if you could spare it."

Judy was stunned . . . she found herself hesitant to do the right thing. She had been influenced by the ladies. Instead of getting the water and food she stood there. Eyes met and the old man waited a few seconds and then silently he turned away. Judy felt ashamed as she went back to the table, but worse was the condemning look from her oldest son.

Quickly she grabbed a pitcher of lemonade, some cookies, and ran out the front door to find the old man on his knees with the children around him listening as he was telling them a Bible story. She offered the cookies and lemonade and told him to wait as she went back to prepare a sack lunch. She returned, "I'm sorry about the way I acted."

"That's all right . . . too many people are influenced by others. But unlike some, you have overcome it and this speaks well for you."

That night Gene had wonderful news! The car he had repaired belonged to a man whose brother ran a repair garage and was looking for a mechanic. He hired Gene on the spot!

Later, Judy told Gene about the events of the afternoon. When finished, he asked, "Did you say this was an elderly black man? Kind looking eyes and gray hair?" He jumped out of bed and went through his pockets until he found a piece of folded paper which he handed to Judy and said, "I met that man walking down the road when I came from town. He waved me over and gave this to me. When I finished reading it, I looked up and he was gone, just disappeared!"

Judy began to cry as she read the note, our verse for today.

Today's Quote: *As much of heaven is visible as we have eyes to see.*
— William Winter

Today's Verse: Do not forget to entertain strangers, for by so doing some people have entertained angels without knowing it (Heb. 13:2).

Day 24
The Delivery Angel

My growing-up years were wonderful and idyllic — a really happy childhood as I look back. It never dawned on me that life was tough at times. My parents at this time were struggling to establish a mission church in the town of Evansville, Minnesota, which had a population of about 850 people, not counting dogs and cats. It was not easy. Dad had to work where he could find a job to support his family . . . it was just him and Mom, my brother 1-1/2 years my junior, and myself. We had a little garden and ate well when some of the church farm families brought goodies to the parsonage. I thought everybody had to live like that . . . the memories of those years are good. It's amazing what time can do to memory.

However . . . one particular night is still a vivid memory. Mom set the table for herself and her two sons. One of us asked, "What are we going to eat tonight?" We looked around, the stove was cold, nothing was on the table except water in the glasses, nothing in the refrigerator, nothing in the cupboards. Not even a potato for watery soup. Not a cup of flour with which to make biscuits. Not even noodles for a hot dish of any kind. The house was bare and two boys were famished!

She said, "Let's sit down and ask the Lord to bless our meal." We dutifully bowed our heads and listened to her prayer. . . .

"Dear Lord, we thank you because you are so good to us. Bless Dad tonight as he's away working. And, Lord, thank you for the food we are about to partake of, in Jesus name I pray . . . " Before she got the final "AMEN" said, both of us heard a noise on the back porch. We shoved our chairs back and in one motion ran for the back door which was about six steps from the kitchen table and flung it open. There, sitting on the porch, were boxes of groceries! We ran out onto the porch and looked in every direction up and down that little dirt street in this little country town where everybody knew everybody and everybody knew everybody else's business. There was nobody! No car, nothing!

With great excitement we hauled the groceries inside, helped Mom put them away until they overflowed the cupboards and the frig! Then we sat down to a glorious feast! We asked, "Mom, who do you think brought the groceries?"

She looked back with a smile and simply said, "Let's just thank the Lord for providing!"

Today's Quote: *Although the span from earth to heaven is a journey of five hundred years, when one whispers a prayer, or even silently meditates, God is nearby and hears.* — Rabbah, an ancient Jewish scholar

Today's Verse: I was young and now I am old, yet I have never seen the righteous forsaken or their children begging bread (Ps. 37:25).

The Emergency Angel

It was a cold early December night in 1990 when Edwin Craig, just newly trained and graduated from the police academy was on duty. He had been assigned to work a patrol at the Denver Airport. As he was making his rounds, he started down a very long deserted walkway/hallway. Quite a ways ahead of him he watched as an older man slowed, stopped, then collapsed and slumped against the wall.

Ed ran quickly to attempt to help the man. He was trying to remember his training as he reached to check a pulse . . . and found none. The man also stopped breathing!

Here it was, his first emergency and he was alone, no backup. He immediately called for medical help on his police radio. The sterile classroom training seemed so long ago. He sensed that if he didn't do something the man would die before help arrived . . . but what to do? What could he do? He breathed a prayer, "Jesus, please help me. Help me to know what to do."

Just then, coming from behind he heard this woman's voice telling him, "I'm an emergency room nurse. I'll do the chest compression if you will do the CPR breathing." Ed was thinking, *Where did she come from, I didn't hear any steps in the hallway.* Steps could have been heard from a long way off echoing . . . but nothing. She was just there.

Edwin began the mouth-to-mouth CPR while she did the chest compressions. When the paramedics arrived and took over, the man began reviving.

"Then," Edwin says, "the most peculiar thing happened. I stood up and looked around for the nurse so I could thank her but she was gone! No one was there! The hallway was long and no exits were handy. She should have been seen easily. She had just appeared out of nowhere when I needed help desperately and when the crisis was over she was gone, vanished!"

Do angels know how to perform CPR? Would an angel have to resort to CPR to revive someone? Well, to this day Edwin Craig believes that angels know CPR! At least one who appeared out of nowhere when needed in Denver. And as a policeman, to this day, he is one cop who now makes his patrols with a sense that there can be divine help in times of need.

Today's Quote: *People have found that science does not have the answers for many of life's problems. While science is helpful in many ways, it just isn't enough.* — Marilynn Carlson Webber

Today's Verse: Jesus did many other miraculous signs in the presence of his disciples, which are not recorded in this book. But these are written that you may believe that Jesus is the Christ, the Son of God, and that by believing you may have life in His name (John 20:30-31).

Day 26
Angel in the Dorm

Evangelist Frankie Walker once told this story to the author.

For a "season" of time I was removed from my traveling ministry and taught in a Bible School, did some counseling, and was a dorm mother to some 20 girls.

One evening I had to leave the girls for about an hour and a half to pick up a lady who was coming from another state to be ordained through our church.

It was an extremely dark night as I drove from the parking lot. As I was a small distance from the dorm, I sensed a strong presence of fear and the thought came, *I cannot leave the girls alone.* I prayed, "Lord, what am I to do? I can't go back, someone has to go to the airport." The Lord impressed me to "charge the angels to guard about the dorm." I did this, committing the safety of the girls to the angels.

On arrival back at the dorm, Pastor Eula and I walked into what should have been a sleeping group of young women. Instead we found the whole group seated on the floor, singing. The girl whom I had put in charge met me at the top of the stairs. "I know we are supposed to be in bed, but allow me to tell you why we are not. After you left, we were visiting when another student came home from work. She said, "Why is Sister Walker standing in her window, curtains open, looking out on the parking lot. She never does that . . . her curtains are always closed at night.' We laughed at her as we explained she must be seeing things because you had gone to the airport."

The girl in charge went on, "We continued talking, then the second carload came from work, three more girls who ride together every day. One of them asked, 'What is Sister Walker doing with her curtains open, watching the parking lot?' " At this, the girls freaked out, some of them frightened to the point of tears.

They decided to check into my room. They found the lights off and drapes closed, just as I had left them. Assured that everything was okay, still shaken, they began to sing and pray together. All of this had been related to me with eyes wide and some tears. Then I explained to them my experience on the road and my instructions to place the angels to guard about them in my absence. I explained the supernatural protection of angels and heard myself say, "That angel looked like me and was guarding you while I was absent."

Today's Quote: *An angel stood and met my gaze, through the low doorway of my tent; the tent is struck, the vision stays; I only know she came and went.* — James Russell Lowell

Today's Verse: So Peter was kept in prison, but the church was earnestly praying to God for him. . . . "You're out of your mind," they told her. When she kept insisting that it was so, they said, "It must be his angel" (Acts 12:5, 15).

The Guardian Angel

A young couple, let's call them Paul and Mary, had struggled with life and as most young couples do, attempted everything they could to scrape together enough money to purchase their first house. Both worked and both were diligent so they could reach their goal. After some years of married life they had enough to purchase a small house on the edge of a modest development. It had one drawback . . . but which also put the purchase price of the house within their reach. The railroad tracks ran across the back of their property. They hesitated, but purchased the house and put up a fence across the back.

Children were soon born into this little family, too. First a son, then a daughter, nearly two years apart in age. The backyard was the favorite outdoors play area . . . sand box, swing set, and a little tree-house. The children were always warned, "Don't leave the backyard and don't go on the railroad tracks!"

Mary was standing at the kitchen sink washing the dishes one glorious spring morning. Just cleaning up after breakfast, Paul had left for work and the two kids were in the back yard. The garden was alive with flowers, rows of carefully planted veggies were peaking up through the soil. The smell of clover filled the air. What a gorgeous day to be alive after the long Minnesota winter had finally passed.

As she looked out, she was suddenly aware that the backyard gate was ajar, open! How? She didn't know. She searched the backyard with her eyes and didn't see the kids! Then she spotted four-year-old Jason . . . sitting casually on the railroad tracks playing with the stones. Two-year-old Melissa was toddling after her big brother and was just starting the climb up to the railway bed. Mary's heart stopped! Panic! Then at almost the same moment . . . she saw the train coming around the bend with whistle blaring. She raced from the house screaming, "Jason! Melissa!" She knew from the nearness of the approaching train and the distance she still had to cover that she would never be able to reach her kids. She shouted a prayer, "Jesus! Jesus! Jesus!"

As she ran shouting, she saw a figure, pure white, striking, and heavenly, lift Jason off the tracks and reach down to grab Melissa. While the train roared past . . . this being, whatever it was, stood by the track with an arm around each child as they watched the train go by.

When the mother reached the tracks, Jason and Melissa were standing alone!

Today's Quote: *Each man (woman or child) has a guardian angel appointed to him.* — Thomas Aquinas

Today's Verse: See that you do not look down on one of these little ones. For I tell you that their angels in heaven always see the face of my Father in heaven (Matt. 18:10).

Angel Provision

Jonathan remembers well his angelic encounter even though it happened over 60 years ago. He was ten years old and the Depression of the thirties was at its peak. He had younger brothers and sisters and it was one horrendous struggle simply to keep food on the table for the family.

One chore which had been assigned to Jonathan was to do the shopping for his mother every Saturday. He would hand the list to the grocer who would help pick out the items on the list. With money in such short supply this was a highly trusted job for such a little boy, but Jonathan did it with pride and a strong sense of responsibility.

On this particular Saturday, his mother gave him the grocery list and tucked ten dollars into his jacket pocket and sent him on his way. She always warned him never to buy anything that was not on the list. When he and the proprietor had loaded his wagon with the groceries from the list he stopped at the counter to pay the lady at the cash register. She asked for the money which was $9.74. He reached into his jacket pocket and no money! Frantic . . . he searched through every pocket . . . in his pants, and through his jacket again . . . no money! He pulled off socks and shoes thinking it may have been there. He looked under his cap . . . he ran back through the store hoping to see it on the floor.

No money! Now filled with panic he began to cry. Nothing to do but leave the groceries and go home to tell his mother. Of course, she was angry and upset . . . to lose $10 in those days was a near catastrophe. There would be nothing to eat this week beyond what had been left in the cupboards. A bleak prospect.

With this Jonathan crept into the basement to cry. He knew what it all meant. As he was sobbing . . . he heard a voice, strong, positive, kind, coming from behind him and it called him by name, "Jonathan, just look into your jacket pocket."

How strange . . . he'd been through the jacket, the clerk at the checkout had been through his jacket, and his mother had searched through the jacket any number of times. How foolish, but he stuck his hand into the pocket once more and there he found the wadded up bills!

And to this day . . . more than 60 years later, whenever discouragement strikes, Jonathan still remembers in the basement when God heard the cries of a little boy and sent a messenger to put ten dollars into a jacket pocket!

Today's Quote: *Come ye blessed children of my Father, receive the kingdom prepared for you from the beginning of the world.* — The Book of Common Prayer

Today's Verse: However, as it is written: "No eye has seen, no ear has heard, no mind has conceived what God has prepared for those who love him" (1 Cor. 2:9).

Day 29
The Comforting Angel

Blanche and Anne ministered as a team of two single ladies in many of the churches of the upper midwest. Blanche was the singer and preacher . . . Anne was the piano player, accompanist, and gal "Friday." They went wherever they were invited — to storefront churches, struggling churches, and large churches, and enjoyed an excellent reputation and were a positive benefit to people wherever they ministered. They traveled back in the days of the extended, protracted meetings . . . two weeks and longer. They were humble, had simple tastes, and were so grateful for all that was done for them in return.

Life was wonderful, ministry was exciting, they were useful and fulfilled in their ministry. BUT that all came to an abrupt halt! Anne was struck down with a stroke! Over a period of time, with rehabilitation she was able to get about with a cane. But the use of her left hand and arm was out of the question . . . no longer could she play the piano, care for herself, or be a contributing factor in ministry.

This left Blanche in a deep quandry. She was frustrated. What to do with life and ministry? How would she support herself? How would Anne support herself? Questions and more questions. Questions that didn't have answers, or at least easy answers.

One night Blanche was lying in bed — reading, pondering, praying, and questioning what God was doing with her and her co-worker's life. She was looking up toward the corner of her bedroom when a small, bright, brilliant, white dot of light appeared. She was drawn to it . . . fascinated. Soon she was able to make out a figure . . . clothed in pure white garments which seemed to shimmer in the light. The figure came closer and closer until it stopped at the foot of the bed. Heavenly! She was awestruck! It simply looked at her with great kindness and exuding love for a period of time, she didn't know how long, and then it was gone!

Later as she reflected on this appearance . . . she was remembering how she seemed to have been flooded with a great sense of well-being. No questions were left to be asked because they were all answered in this personal appearance! Blanche says she has never questioned the happenings nor change of direction for her life as well as Anne's.

The songwriter has penned a simple line, "One glimpse of His dear face, all sorrows will erase. . . ."

Today's Quote: *I also believe in angels because I have sensed their presence in my life on special occasions.* — Billy Graham

Today's Verse: Our mouths were filled with laughter, our tongues with songs of joy. Then it was said among the nations, "The Lord has done great things for them." The Lord has done great things for us, and we are filled with joy. Restore our fortunes, O Lord (Ps. 126:2-3).

Day 30
Rachael's Angel

Rachael recently had a nightmarish experience and lived to tell the story. As she was returning to her car which was parked at the mall she was accosted by two men, who at gunpoint forced her into their car. They blindfolded her and hurriedly drove out to a deserted woods where she was raped. Before her attackers left, one of them drew out the gun and shot her three times and fled.

Several hours had passed, she had no recollection of how many . . . but somehow she started to revive and managed to struggle to her feet. She futilely searched for her shoes and couldn't find them. In her bare feet she fell, stumbled, walked, crawled out to the country road. She knew that if she were to get some help, she'd have to walk the miles to town. With her goal in focus . . . she began to make her way on the harsh gravel of the roadway, stopping frequently to rest. She would walk and fall, then sit for a while to gather some strength and get up to go again. She feared she would die before she found help.

She began to pray and asked God to please send someone to help her. In her weakened state, and near delirious with pain and loss of blood, she all of a sudden felt like she was being helped along — almost like being carried and she didn't stumble and fall anymore. Finally she reached the first house on the edge of town and at that moment it seemed as if she were placed gently back on the ground.

There was a light on in the house . . . so she managed to walk up the three steps onto the porch and knocked on the door. A young woman answered . . . took one long look at Rachael and crumpled to the floor in a dead faint. Her husband stepped over his wife to help Rachael inside to a couch on which to lie down. He quickly phoned 911 for an ambulance then went back to help his wife who was beginning to revive. When she was back functioning and seated in a chair across from the couch, Rachael somehow managed a wan smile said, "I'm sorry that I frightened you like this. I know I must look terrible."

The wife replied, "No, that's not why I fainted. I saw this great shining angel holding you up as you stood in the doorway!"

Later at the emergency room of the hospital where the ER doctor examined her he noted that even though she had gunshot wounds and bruises from the rape . . . and had covered several miles on the rough gravel road, there was not even a scratch or bruise on her bare feet!

Today's Quote: *I also believe in angels because I have sensed their presence in my life on special occasions.* — Billy Graham

Today's Verse: The Egyptians mistreats us and our fathers, but when we cried out to the Lord, He heard our cry and sent an angel and brought us out of Egypt" (Num. 20:15-16).

Notes

1. Billy Graham, *Angels: God's Secret Agents* (Irving, TX: Word, Inc., 1991).
2. Hope MacDonald, *When Angels Appear* (Grand Rapids, MI: Zondervan Publishing House, 1995), page 41-42.
3. Kenneth Nordvall; James S. Hewett, editor, *Illustrations Unlimited* (Wheaton, IL: Tyndale House Publishers, 1988).
4. Joan Webster Anderson, *Where Miracles Happen* (New York, NY: Ballantine Books, Random House, Inc., 1994), page 104-106.
5. Jan Winebrenner, *Steel in His Soul: The Dick Hillis Story* (Milpitas, CA: Overseas Crusades, 1985).
6. Charles Treptow, *Parables, Etc., 12/95*.

Moments to Give series

Available at bookstores nationwide or write
New Leaf Press, P.O. Box 726, Green Forest, AR 72638